Beyond Me

BEYOND ME

VOICES OF THE NATURAL WORLD

Poetry by Margaret Holley

Photography by Christine Safford Beck

NORTHWORD
PRESS, INC

Minocqua, Wisconsin

Acknowledgments

DYLAN THOMAS: POEMS OF DYLAN THOMAS.
Copyright © 1945 by the Trustees for the Copyrights of
Dylan Thomas. Reprinted by permission of New
Directions Publishing Corp.

Marianne Moore: Reprinted by permission of
Macmillan Publishing Company from COLLECTED
POEMS OF MARIANNE MOORE. Copyright © 1944,
renewed 1972, by Marianne Moore.

Edited by Greg Linder
Designed by Patricia Bickner Linder

Published by: NorthWord Press, Inc.
               PO Box 1360
               Minocqua, WI 54548

Library of Congress Cataloging-in-Publication Data

Holley, Margaret.
    Beyond me / by Margaret Holley.
        p.   cm.
    ISBN 1-55971-215-5 : $17.95
    1. Nature--Poetry.   I. Title
PS3558.034964B4   1993
811'.54--dc20   93–10985
                                       CIP

For a free color catalog offering NorthWord's complete
line of nature books and gifts, call 1-800-336-5666.

Printed in Singapore

Contents

The Unbeaten Path

The way that can be spoken of
is not the eternal way.
The name that can be named
is not the eternal name.

Lao-tzu

My first knowledge was following
everywhere you went,
understanding nothing

but your presence, your voice,
the warm world of your body
waking me gradually.

Then it opened ahead of me, too,
        paved with footprints, past
                and future—the picture of time:

a still river moving
        through the dappled thickets
                of each moment, this clearing

at my feet that gives me
        the feeling of going somewhere
                and sends my heart ahead.

Eventually I, too,
        (this was nothing new) had to
                leave the narrow path,

the one made to stray from,
        looking like Eden on all sides,
                until you actually enter.

I saw the meadow where
　　　someone turns to strike the child,
　　　　　　the meadow where families stand

at gunpoint, meadows of fire
　　　filled with children of the sun
　　　　　　with darkness blooming in them.

Some roads less travelled
　　　have taken me higher, taken
　　　　　　more out of me than I'd dreamed,

wearied me with the sheer weight
　　　of myself. Call it a way
　　　　　　of defying the gravities

of this globe, washing my head
　　　in clouds and the clarity
　　　　　　of their great blue sea.

Oh father, how many mansions
        there are in the heavens
                into which you have vanished

all around me! The warm world,
        your body, wakes me gradually
                past all understanding.

~

Calyx, Chalice

I felt myself dying,
cracking, falling apart,
losing my mind,

and I was afraid.
My whole body was made of dread,
stiffening, splitting

into a hundred pieces,
memories, dreams, the wildest
of my tears and wishes,

bud-shaped, tender,
saying now, let go, let go,
we are going for the sun.

~

Little Mind, Big Mind

Do not seek to follow in the footsteps
of the men of old; seek what they sought.

Matsuo Basho

What I need is beyond me, where I think
I have never been before.

I walk toward it, half-blinded by beauty
on all sides:

weed, stream, waterfall, rainbow and mist.
I carry a child,

a wild thing wounded, a riot of dreams,
clamor of wishes

rarely quiet enough to hear what is coming
down the river of wind.

I lay my weight on stone with one foot,
then the other,

a form of prayer, earthbound, earthbound:
alpha and old omega,

my wide captivity, my last destination.
I clamber up and up

its shoulder, labor headlong into height,
drinking distance in,

feeling the breezes enter and wash freely
through cell and bone,

wearing blown ash and pollen in my hair
without noticing them.

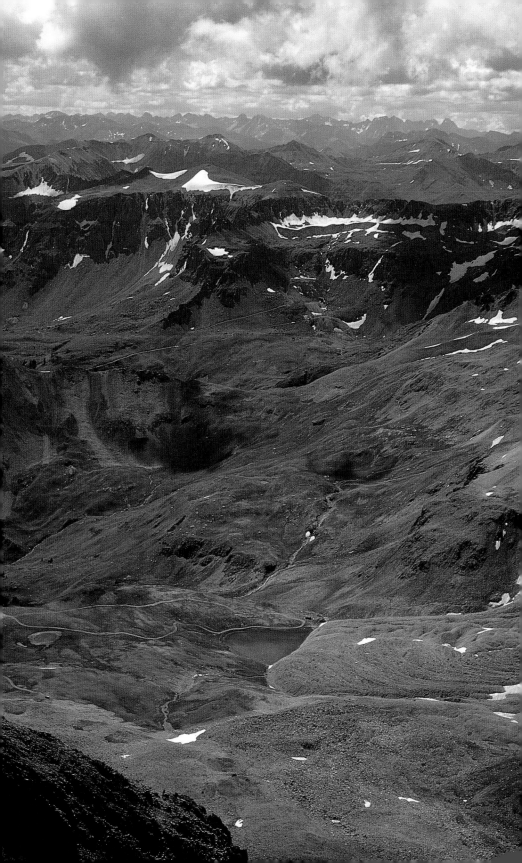

I climb up past all plans and preparations
and reasons why,

till my own life seems so small and far away
I can't find it any more,

and each bootprint behind me is someone's
I used to be,

and my mind is as still as the mountains,
and I am their speech.

~

Born

My maker is the rising wind.
My body is water, dust,
dressed in sunlight,
even by the moon.

My body is an island
in the sea of the unseen.
My maker is the thought of change.
My name is Vanishing.

My spirit is all my children,
born and unborn.
You dream my dreams for me.
My name is Hope.

~

Lilies

The force that through the green fuse drives the flower
Drives my green age.

Dylan Thomas

i.

Out of the nowhere in our midst
come the leaves, growing as we grow

(palm, fingers, branching of veins,
nucleotides dreaming in trillions),

green inheriting the earth again
each spring. Only one sunlit speck

in the whole night blizzard,
as far as we know, wakes in this way

to warmth, works in the plural
by such radical means, fur and satin,

the sun-drenched pond, each
crowded kingdom within a kingdom

repeating itself with saving mistakes,
multiplying hunger by itself

to share one rootbed, earth's
sweet crust and teeming waters:

so many faces lifted to the sun,
one loaf, one fish to feed us all.

ii.

And then to find there is no such thing
in the world as one. Only one world

beyond and within, pausing and moving on,
each creature continuous with its mud.

I am an estuary, a pooling of streams,
a conspiracy of soil and sunlight.

The two clouds I carry around my heart
only borrow the air momentarily.

I raise shelter, seeds; I will turn myself
into the velvet muck of the pond floor.

Having made me up, now it wants to use
my eyes, my hands, whatever leaves

I may have grown in the shape of a heart.
And one buttercup sun,

one bowl of light

sticks its neck out, lifting its head
over water visible only in its shining,

and consents on my behalf, "Yes,
open me up, take whatever you need."

~

Blue Columbine

I am a star that goes with thee
and shines out of the depths.

Mithraic proverb

i. The Flower Sermon

"I cannot tell you how
it led from silence to silence
through a river of tears,
the single bloom held up so quietly
between the Buddha's fingers.

We had asked him for teaching,
loving to hear him speak,
but he said nothing,
held quite still,
as the petals caught a breeze

and understanding welled up
audibly through me,
setting me down
upon another shore,
where I heard for the first time

the wind's breath
playing the things of the world:
his body, a hillside in bloom,
the stem of his arm,
this sermon going on and on."

ii. Seeds

Where is it now, my pretty pinwheel,
my lavender silk and lily white,
my bright bouquet?
Where is it now
in this city of ice,

this empire of the dying?
What lasts forever is what vanishes
and returns.
But I am afraid
I can't see more than one generation

at a time.
A long time ago
among Roman legions
loud with armor and dirty
with marching, indulgence, and slaves,

Mithras, god of light,
touched his foot to earth
and baptized them with water
saying "I am a star,"
the mirror of your soul,

I am the mind of the mountain,
the heart of the flower,
stars at your feet,
the spirit I love in you
rising up out of common clay.

iii. Starflower

Sweet earth gathers up the gone
and goes on raising
lanterns: buttery poppies,
Jacob's ladder, and columbine,
the lotus of the hills.

Its gold and white light
travels all nights—
blindness, the back of the mind,
even Egypt, the old bondage
to which I have so often fled,

its stones starred with hieroglyphs,
where the five-pointed star
meant "rising upward"
and appeared in the pictures
for "educate" and "teacher."

Star within star
opens over the mud, the mess,
the overcrowded Bethlehem I am,
when I no longer think I know
how to live

and finally grow quiet enough
to hear what the heart repeats
and repeats, its lifelong whisper:
teach me, teach us all
in time.

~

Flame

Bring me my bow of burning gold,
Bring me my arrows of desire.

William Blake

Doubtful,
disbelieving,
ever in need of signs,

I stand
in the bright meadow
like Moses, arguing my inadequacies,

while an angel
flames and flickers
in the green patience of the bush.

Oh, wisdom
beyond the eyes,
take me through time

into the mind
and heart of Heraclitus
as he studied the stones of Ephesus,

scrolls
of river water
hurrying over his feet,

and concluded
that everything, every
thing in the world is fire,

"ever-living Fire,
in measures being kindled
and in measures going out."

Come, voice
of the invisible wind
to my inner ear, come

angel-flame,
burn in my meadow,
burn in the darkness of my heart.

~

Heartwood

A tree whose hungry mouth is prest
Against the earth's sweet flowing breast . . .

"Trees" by Joyce Kilmer,
Sergeant of the 165th Infantry,
killed in action, July 30, 1918.

From the classroom into the mud
of France, he carried the vision
of beauty as wood nymph,

"a nest of robins in her hair,"
and fell, armed and helmeted,
to "earth's sweet flowing breast."

New sapwood, soft tissue
ringing the trunk year by year,
lifts rain back up its halls:

whole forests of water fountain up
each spring, unfolding leaves,
petals, engorging fruit,

each tree lifting its head
higher, opening its arms wider,
as it rises around its old self.

Old heartwood, dead center
of the living tree, the core
of old saplings overgrown,

learns the ever gentler lean
of holding still: let the last
leaves go, remain in place,

and prepare to do it all again
on a larger scale. Each summer
draws its dark line in the stem,

memory gathering in its strength,
defining backbone as knowing
just how much to sway.

Alone, and never alone,
solitary, never singular,
we make our brief appearances

in a mist of wishful thinking,
growing and dying at once—
sapwood, heartwood, deadwood,

wrinkling, knotting at the joints,
stooping with the burden
of complexity—sweetness and grief,

the nerveweb of honeysuckle,
thicket of ivy, pelt of mosses,
and rain trickling down the trunk.

Old rotund mother earth
with both arms around us, nursing
and crushing, bearing, burying—

Ghostly father, trying to make
love of another kind out of us—
who made whom? Are you ever

one and the same power?—
soil, water, and sun raising
their aging broods and the spirit's

quest to be more than the beast
it rides. We have dreamed
our dreams of glory,

of Igdrasil, the cosmic tree
with stars for fruit, found it
rooting in our own back yard

in a nest of snow, twigs, leaves,
and marchbells, and ripped it out.
We have used her like a whore,

and she takes us all,
trunk and fur and fallen birds,
the slain soldiers, the crucified,

back to her breast, letting
the children suckle and climb
for sunshine, letting us try again.

~

Kea Bird

What I see
is little, so small
a part of all
that is,
yet how swiftly

it brings
the invisible
—wind, birdcall,
memory—
on its wings.

~

One River

The quality of mercy is not strained,
It droppeth as the gentle rain from heaven
Upon the place beneath.

William Shakespeare

One river, many names.
Cloud, snow, mist, ocean, dew.
And deity's grace, transparency:

"Take this world as if
it were your own forever."
I am history, a long shoreline,

a memory of descent
from thighs of ice
and the tropics of spring,

a pilgrimage through pine woods,
when I forget everything
I knew of the future.

I am complete craziness,
making my dance
out of the quietness of stones,

flying up over them
on my way down,
letting them all shine.

And days of leisure,
the sky almost holding still
in the back of my mind.

Always I dream canyons
and carry my shores away with me
grain by grain.

A thousand tributaries,
one great delta pushing its fan
of brown silt into the ocean.

I remember fish
flocking like birds
through my deep blue.

Finally I am a single drop
flying free over the falls.
Oh, beautiful world!

And my body is made of it!
I fall and fall
slowly through the years,

images turning in me as I go,
whole forests in one teardrop.
And look at me now,

a translucent pool
of jade and amethyst,
a small whirl laced with memory,

faces, voices, places with names.
It won't last long,
and then I'll be sleepy again,

but I see it, I see
one river branching
like an ancient tree

with its arms around the earth,
around us all,
saying I baptize you

every day, this is my blood
flowing every day,
this is the gentle rain.

~

Wildflower

Entreat me not to leave thee,
nor to turn back from following thee.

Ruth 1:16

You came as a stranger
into the land of Moab,
and I as a stranger have come

to Judah. In drought
and famine, the desert
reduces everything to bone.

In love and grief
the alien tongues become
our own. Because I loved you,

because I love you,
the strangeness of it all
takes root in me and blooms:

Bethlehem, moonlight
over a high tide of barley.
My chosen family, my friend,

who I am with you
is a world beyond myself,
and where I am with you is home.

~

Lichens, Stone

*The weak overcomes its
menace, the strong over-
comes itself.*

Marianne Moore

i. Lichens

Blue-green algae
bedded down with clear,
brown, gold, or rust-red fungi:
the world's most tender mouths
suckle on stone
where the bones of the earth
show through,

nurse on the cold shoulder
of the boulder's atomic universe,
take the exact shape
of each of the emerging grains
and the spaces in between,
breaking it down
into plain new dirt.

I am young, too,
an infant riding a slow wave
of the ancient sea
of rock, as it pretends to be
unchanging. What a strange place!
Where insisting appears
as giving in.

Who is the firm
and who the yielding here?
And yet I can live on this.
What are years to me
with this taste on my tongue?
Pure earth and its possibilities,
the galaxies within.

ii. Stone

Whatever world you come from,
how could you have known
I wasn't so adamant?
I had tired of my hard heart
and its helplessness,
of not knowing how to be
anything else.

I have lain here for years
silent in storms, in snow,
in the oven of sun,
dreaming sadly
of your small and tender mouths
saying nothing, dissolving,
absolving all.

Wherever you come from
I'm ready to go,
though I can't think how.
Perhaps I'm starting to learn,
or I'm already partly there,
being taken slowly
to pieces, even my fear.

Let it be my turn now
to be transformed,
to wake from this sleep.
Make me into soil,
deepen in me the invisible world
where root hairs drink
at the clear wells of rain.

~

Evergreen

. . . and the leaves of the tree
were for the healing of the nations.

Revelations 22:2

Forty-six centuries the oldest of these have spent
learning the shapes of the wind,
learning to bow just the way the wind wishes,
slow partners in the dance of air around the turning world.

All generations of sapling now suckling at the stony breast
are children of its years,
each with its twin rooting invisibly
into another world that is the just depth of this one.

The wind makes one song into everyone's,
makes it rise and travel, heavy with ash and radiant plumes,
to wrap the earth in cries and babel and after-quiet
that hum in the veins of the unfolding leaves.

Through these branches echoed the blows of Egypt hammering
outcropping rock into a lion's body with a man's head,
the voice of the poet of Babylon singing
of Gilgamesh the king weeping for his friend.

Through their branches moved the thoughts
of Siddhartha sitting in darkness under the fig tree,
and the lengthening, listening pause of a young carpenter
planing blond curls from the wood of Galilee.

Do you think what you say is not heard,
makes no difference? Even your silence is gathered
into the breathing spaces between things. The whole grove,
growing sotto voce, branches out into new meanings of evergreen

with the voice of rain whispering hymns, dreaming seeds
in the little tree of the cone, the shape of things to come:

Now I lay me down, so slowly, taking forever, still
lifting my candles into the wordless wind.

~

Pure Gold

The alchemist's goal
of making base metals into gold
is a parable of the soul.

M. H.

The alchemy of ferns
in woods and window pots
aims, not at what stays,
but at what returns:

what consents to go brown,
to rot, and the wet blackness
that comes back as saffron,
lemon, jasmine, and cream,

essence of leafmold
unfolding the bud, scenting
the rose. The greedy wind
takes everything away,

and a root says, "It's okay,
I can grow some more,"
patience as faith
making the desert bloom.

So it gleams and goes:
birch in October
dappling mud with coins,
the sun coming uncurtained,

suddenly spilling light
spun out of varnished pine
into inner space, filling
the whole room. Grace.

~

Mysteries

House made of dawn,
House made of evening light...

Navaho chant

Night rises out of the ground,
and dreams rise up around me
on all sides like acquaintances
whose names I cannot recall,

and the last gold of afternoon
glints like stars in the grass.
Small emissaries dart and sing
in the air, preparing to travel

the rainbow again, its rosy pinks
and amber, the pale green horizon,
aquamarine of the sea of air.
Then the long sonata in blue,

twilight's deepening indigos
and india ink, the lace of trees,
staining the world out there
I sometimes think of as my mind.

Goodbye, my sweet busy oblivion.
Soon I have another rendezvous
to lie down in the dark meadow
and attend its endless mysteries.

~

Unborn

This moment in the sun
will be the end of me.
It is already time
to be something else.

My name? It is your name.
My body is a memory
afloat in your eyes.
Like me, you sail

the sea of the unseen.
Ship full of gold,
where are you going
with treasure in your hold?